Star Patterns

Written by Alison Milford

Illustrated by Ángeles Peinador

Collins

On a clear night, you will spot clusters of glittering stars. Some star clusters look like living things.

A springing goat with a fishtail!

A creeping crab!

3

The best star cluster to spot is the hunter! His belt has three stars. Near his left foot is a bright star.

This is part of his dog. It is speeding off to hunt a rabbit.

This cluster looks like a pair of swooshing fish. A cord of stars connects them.

Some star clusters can be spotted at just one point in the year. On summer nights, you might spot this creeping fox.

On winter nights, look for this trail of stars.

If you join up this twisting string of stars, you will spot a serpent!

Some think it is coiled on to the waist of a man.

It is fun looking for patterns in star clusters.

I spot a little frog!

There are lots to spot!

I spot a bright snail!

13

What patterns can you spot?

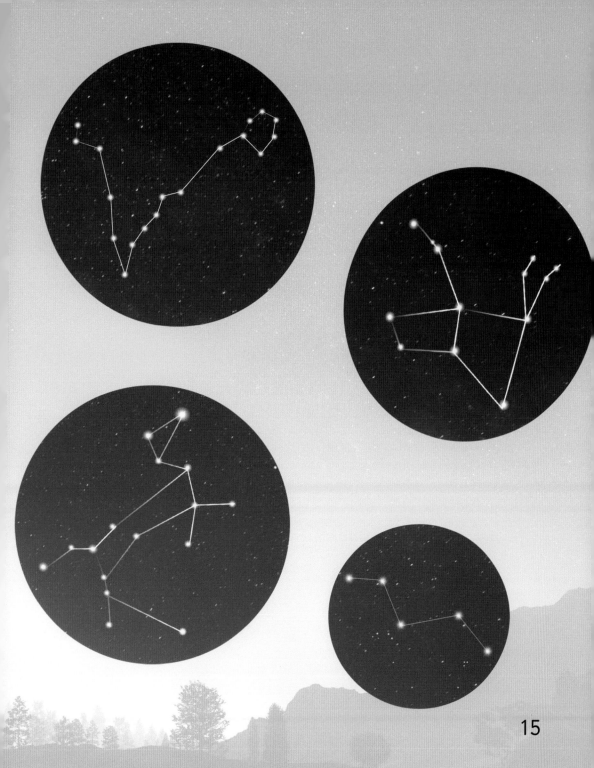

 Review: After reading

Use your assessment from hearing the children read to choose any GPCs, words or tricky words that need additional practice.

Read 1: Decoding

- Turn to page 10 and reread the sentence. Ask: What does the word **string** mean here? Discuss how it means a line – a line of stars that you can join up.
- Focus on words with adjacent consonants and long vowel sounds. Ask the children to sound out these words. Explain that they can split the words into chunks or syllables to help sound them out.

  speed/ing   creep/ing   float/ing   swoosh/ing

- Point to speech bubbles and ask the children if they can read them out fluently, like real spoken words. Say: Can you do any blending in your head instead of out loud?

Read 2: Prosody

- Discuss with the children how they would read pages 6 and 7 for a radio recording. Ask: Would you use the same voice to read pages 6 and 7? (*no, e.g. the voices on page 7 should be children's*)
- Model reading the main text on page 6 in a serious broadcaster's voice, and the speech bubbles on page 7 in an excited tone.
- Challenge the children to read the pages in pairs, using the appropriate voices.

Read 3: Comprehension

- Ask the children: What did you already know about stars? Do you know anything that isn't covered in this book?
- Turn to pages 2 and 3 and reread the text. Ask: Is there really a picture of a crab in the sky? Is it real? If necessary, point out the phrase **look like** on page 2, and explain that the pictures are imagined.
- Challenge the children to think of alternative words or phrases with a similar meaning for these words. For each choice, ask the children to read back the sentence to see if it makes sense.
  - page 6: **cluster** (e.g. *group, bunch*) page 10: **twisting** (*wavy, curled*) page 13: bright (e.g. *shining, light*) page
  - Turn to the cover and ask: Is there a word we can use instead of **Patterns**? (e.g. *shapes, pictures*) Ask: Which word do you like best? Why?
- Turn to pages 14 and 15. Ask the children to talk about the patterns they can see. Can they remember any from the book?